Chrysalis Summer

Poems of Transformation

Suzanne Brody

Teaneck, New Jersey

Published by Ben Yehuda Press
122 Ayers Court #1B
Teaneck, NJ 07666
BenYehudaPress.com

To subscribe to our monthly book club and support independent Jewish publishing, visit https://www.patreon.com/BenYehudaPress

Jewish Poetry Project #42   **http://jpoetry.us**

Ben Yehuda Press books may be purchased at a discount by synagogues, book clubs, and other institutions buying in bulk. For information, please email markets@BenYehudaPress.com

Cover image was created using Generative AI tools including ChatGPT, Copilot, and Adobe Photoshop.

ISBN13 978-1-963475-33-3 pb 978-1-963475-34-0 epub

Library of Congress Cataloging-in-Publication Data

Names: Brody, Suzanne, 1976- author.
Title: Chrysalis summer : poems of transformation / Suzanne Brody.
Description: Teaneck, New Jersey : Ben Yehuda Press, 2024. | Series: The
  Jewish poetry project ; #42 | Summary: ""Chrysalis Summer" by Suzanne
  Brody is a collection of poetry that delves into the transformative
  experiences of growth, education, and personal relationships. Through a
  series of poignant and reflective poems, Brody explores themes of
  learning, spiritual exploration, and the nuances of human connections,
  set against the backdrop of seasonal change"-- Provided by publisher.
Identifiers: LCCN 2024017680 (print) | LCCN 2024017681 (ebook) | ISBN
  9781963475333 (trade paperback) | ISBN 9781963475340 (epub)
Subjects: LCSH: Change--Poetry. | LCGFT: Poetry.
Classification: LCC PS3602.R6359 C48 2024 (print) | LCC PS3602.R6359
  (ebook) | DDC 811/.6--dc23/eng/20240507
LC record available at https://lccn.loc.gov/2024017680
LC ebook record available at https://lccn.loc.gov/2024017681

24 25 26 / 10 9 8 7 6 5 4 3 2   20240803

Dedicated to
those who hold space for us to test our wings

Wandering My Way

For all those traveling these paths with me, "Maybe you have to know the darkness before you can appreciate the light."

– Madeleine L'Engel

Chrysalis Summer

In the heat of July
I begin to emerge
blinking
in the strong light
of returning hope.
I remain
rooted
slowly freeing myself
from emotional tangles
and testing relationships
ready
to begin wandering
on the path
to becoming myself.

Rooted

Stepping Stones

We line our garden
with a rainbow
of values,
finding paths
through the mind
into heart and soul.
We tug on collective memory,
sending up prayers
on wings of song
as we skip
from one lesson
to another.

 Suzanne Brody

Sammy Educator

I watched in fascination
as colorful images
and torrents of words
were tossed
into the ether
sometimes followed
by a flurry of cash.
"Mentor," I asked
"what are they doing?"
"Advertising jobs,"
 came the reply.
"Can I post a job?"
"Silly little educator,"
 came the reply
"Educators
 don't blindly post,
 Educators
 build webs
 and tug on the strings
 one at a time
 until we catch
 just the right one
 to get the job done
 Right."

Moral Meaning in Our Work

We use
the words of our ancestors
and cries of souls
throughout time and space
as tools
growing
a community
that cares
to make the world better
for each other.

 Suzanne Brody

Seussian Emotions

You can breathe
anywhere
in the car
outside the door
before the meeting
in front of class
publicly
or privately
deep lungfuls
of sanity.

Growing Souls Together

You provide the soil
for my garden
and she
scatters seeds
that he blesses
while another
sings the melody
that wakes up
the one in the corner
and you
add a scaffold
that one needs to thrive.
We are in the business
of growing souls
never knowing
what will sprout
under whose guidance
or which essential ingredient
our partners might bring
at just the right time.
So we walk together
offering our pearls
and letters of fire
as we issue unique calls
and souls reply
each in their own voice.

 Suzanne Brody

When's Snack?

They walk through the doors
cavernous pits
still digesting breakfast
eager
not for the games planned
art projects prepped
stories to be shared
but
already anticipating
knowing
this is a place
that nourishes
the physical, too.

Glitter

It's been four weeks
since laughter
bounced off these walls
and bodies careened
from one idea to another.
The broom and vacuum
have come and gone
more times than they can count
but glitter still sparkles
in unexpected places
waiting
for next year's students.

                    Suzanne Brody

Shape of Education

The future
is built
from triangles
and circles
deceptively simple
to cut through the noise
and focus
on the core
that will move us forward.

Revolutionary Evolution

Lifesaving mutations
Maintaining
Hugs of tradition.

          Suzanne Brody

Educator's Sole

Worn down
from chasing the perfect combination
of engagement for all
yet still with enough
life and bounce
to be patched
with playdough
and evidence of snack
fueling minds
who decorate the world
in glitter, stickers
and ideas.

Soul of an Educator

The soul of an educator
doesn't need a building
or fancy structure
with a fence
that keeps out more than it protects.
The soul of an educator
thrives
sharing pieces of itself
with others.

                    Suzanne Brody

The 10 Senses

Beyond the 5
they teach in kindergarten
lurk another 5,
imagination
soul
connections
personal synesthesia
and the magic mystery
we can't quite define,
or maybe
there's an infinite unfolding
of ways we encounter
our own worlds.

Who is Wise?

Being wise
isn't about
what you know
but about
how wide
you are willing
to crack open
and let yourself
be filled
with someone else's thoughts
as a bridge
to the future.

               Suzanne Brody

In Relationships

Supermom Attempt

My red cape
looks more like
a green square
around a white telephone.
The only part of me
traveling at super speed
is my voice,
and I cannot
really be
in two places at once
no matter
how hard I try
to dry your eyes
while simultaneously
being miles away
here in this chair.

Love Manifesto

Maybe one day
you'll finally feel
the web of love
I've spun around you
since time before
with longings and proddings
through the kidney kicks
and powder sweet
becoming stinky feet,
from the microscopic
to the taller than me.
Maybe one day
you'll finally feel
the love woven
in treats offered,
attempts to understand
the fantasy worlds
behind your screen
and outstretched arms.
Then maybe
you'll finally
let yourself
feel supported
and cherished.

Rabbi's Child

I feel their eyes
judging
my every move
their lips
discussing, dissecting
piling up moments
they see bad behavior
undisciplined
wild
inappropriate
and in my mind
I hear them
uncomprehending
yet passing sentence anyway.
But sometimes
I think I see a glimmer
of utter compassion
sympathy for the struggles
openness to learning
our challenges.

          Suzanne Brody

Broken?

What do you do
when someone's
social-emotional wheel
is full of holes
and the patches fall off
no matter which ones
or how many
you apply
year after year?

Becoming Equal

Neither an eraser
nor a pencil
are enough
to rebalance
our world.
Finding egalitarianism
is not forcing one
into the mold of the other
but crafting
a new reality
that still feels
like the weight
of tradition.

          Suzanne Brody

Breach

Jeremiah lamented
"Then a breach was made
in the city"
and still
its walls
assaulted by rockets
and its air
split
by the sound of sirens
reverberating
in my heart
miles away
and I found
the cry of my soul
buried
in ancient text
opened
like comforting arms
when I needed it most.
A confirmation
of all I believe
like a rainbow
in the storm.

Portrait of a Woman

Through a maze of mirrors
reflecting in male eyes
she looks and acts
like a slave
with no property
of her own,
a living extension
of her husband.
But turn a bit
and we find
an independent
person in her own right
not at all
like a slave.

                    Suzanne Brody

Moses

Reluctant to assume
the mantle of leadership
feeling defined by a deficit,
unaware of our own strength
to kill with one hit
and split rocks
with taps meant for emphasis,
we are brought low
for failure
to channel power
through words
instead of actions.

Grasshopper Feelings

There's no need
to throw the baby out
or even
change the water
when some bubbles
or temperature adjustment
would be enough.
There's no need
to fan the flames
and pull us
over coals
while throwing out
the shoes I made.
I'd gladly
show you the pattern,
explain the path I made
while pointing out
the thorns too tough
to uproot
and the hidden gems
waiting to be found.
There's no need
for you to feed
my grasshopper feelings
in this season of change

          Suzanne Brody

Her Hand

Her hand
covered with lines
that speak her life,
the scar acquired in childhood
nails trimmed and buffed
stained with berry juice
belongs
to him
to do with
as he wishes
so he carries it
wherever he goes.

Usufruct

Peach juice
sticks to his chin
as he cups a plum
in the palm of his hand
and her pursed lips
don't taste
his legal plunder
of her childhood garden.

 Suzanne Brody

Unsent Email

My best
will never be
good enough
for you.
Even
your praise
holds criticism
and you
are wringing me dry
trying to shove
your vision
down my throat
and control me
like a puppet.
But I am reaching
for my strength
and when my wings unfurl
who knows what I can do.

Threatened Supervisor?

Would you feel
like a squashed ant
if you acknowledged
my ideas and plans
have value, too?
Would your mind
go spinning into darkness
if my tone of voice
felt like a constant rebuke?
Would you dissolve
into a salty, soggy mess
if occasional validation
crossed your lips?
Does recognition
that I possess wisdom
and experience
cause you pain and nausea?
Would admission
of the hours and energy
I expend
lessen your weariness and exhaustion?
Would it hurt you
to see me
succeed
on my own terms?

   Suzanne Brody

Wandering Sheep

I'm constantly striving
to be the best shepherd
this flock has ever seen,
leading my sheep
to deep pastures
they thought they'd never enjoy
but even Moses
had sheep who wandered off
who only thrived
with unconventional tending
and I
never claimed to be a Moses.

A Reincarnated Yalta

Your words are arrows
flying in all directions
spilling feelings
like Yalta spilled the wine,
escalating and compounding
insults and accusations
even if we all agree
they started it first.

    Suzanne Brody

Cain and Abel

Maybe
God is a picky eater
a vegetarian
who leaves the meat
pushed aside.
Maybe
God never learned
about no-thank-you helpings
and trying a bite
without
yucking someone else's yum.
Maybe
God hadn't yet realized
how humans react
when they feel rejected.

Passing

The space between
life and death
is the time that it takes
for the last synapse
to fire
and the final
wisp of breath
to leave the nose.

                    Suzanne Brody

Hidden

Is it derailing our class
if I refuse
to let myself
be run over
by the views you espouse?
Instead
I've gone undercover
not revealing
my credentials,
choosing
to let you
wear the mantle of authority
and secretly wishing
my true self
to be unmasked
and acknowledged.

Untangled

Tying yourself
to the branches
of the tree
heavy with fruit
satisfying your hunger
does not
prevent her
from selling the yard
that nurtures this tree
even
if you are married.

 Suzanne Brody

Collegial Therapy

Here by the waves
I am heard
and reminded
I am not alone.
There are others
who understand
all the turmoil
triangles and circles
are able to cause
when we are speaking
with those
not used to listening.

Diagnosis

We thought it was
repeated hits
shaking us all
to the core
getting buried
by the bricks
we thought we needed
to rebuild
the past
but the problem
is really
dried out shock absorbers
and trouble seeing
a new way forward.

 Suzanne Brody

Lifeboat

I cannot
repair the ship
I did not steer
into the rocks
but I can
reach out my hand
to help you
onto the lifeboat
and together
we'll find a place
to grow.

Potion Effectiveness

My anti-demon potion
of oils and dyes
spread on wood pulp
in cryptic runes
is not potent enough
today
to ward off
salt-water sprayer
and nasty thought twisters.

 Suzanne Brody

Wandering My Way

No a la Carte

God
is not
a vending machine
and life
is not
a restaurant
where you can order
what you want
not even with bribes
bills piled high
and the dressing
does not come on the side
with fries instead of onion rings
but you get
what you need
even if
you never know it
ten years later.

 Suzanne Brody

Stolen Holiness

I have fought with the water
and the eyes
I thought
were watching
my every flaw.
I have floated
in the candlelight
surrounded by words
kissing my soul.
And tonight
I have stolen holiness.

Presenter

He is speaking my life
and I find myself
in definitions and stories
telling me
this path
has been worn down
by other feet before
and like them
I can
discover a way
through the darkness.

              Suzanne Brody

Un-Enslavement

Money is a tool
that never belongs
to you,
it passes through
each of us
to release you
from those
keeping us from freedom.

Return

Familiar names
now form a maze,
snatches of memories
a lifetime old
not enough
to redraw the map
with updated construction
even
as a feeling of home rises
from the stones
through my feet
to my heart.

 Suzanne Brody

Magnetism

Every legal code
dressed in tuxedos
with crisp lines
and clear boundaries
attracts
flamboyant commentaries
eager to create gray
add polka dots
and wrap us all
in splashes of color.

Jewish Twilight

Jewish twilight
belongs
to two days,
the past and the future
suspended
in the uncertainty
that is both
day and night
where if we look
we can find the twinkling lights
to pull us forward
into the darkness
in the hopes
of finding
new treasures.

 Suzanne Brody

Finding Safe Space

A cocoon
of blankets and pillows
provides a retreat
where feelings
of being crushed
or suffocated
find me
and even if
I could run or fly
as fast as my dreams
of the greatest superheroes
my baggage
never stays lost
for long.
But a seat by the shore
is its own type of magic.

Spiritual Technology

Discretionary goodness
layered with temporary
permanence
exposed dichotomies
stretched into revealing
nuance unpacked
words
freed from the page

          Suzanne Brody

Past Influences

The past
whispers in my ear
trying to influence
future decisions
whether as a road block
or encouraging cheerleader
I can't quite tell.

Moving

What do we pack
in the boxes we bring
into our future?

 Suzanne Brody

Leaves' Journey

The leaves want the ground
in autumn
tired
and sunburnt
after
a summer spent
painting the sky green
waiting
to be covered
by a soft white blanket
nestled
under a sparking
reflection in the heavens.

Before Leaping

Standing
on the edge
of a cliff

leaning forward
anticipating
something amazing
but held in place
by tangles of fear
indecision
and fingers that feel
much like my own.

                    Suzanne Brody

Ancient Advice

Lot's wife
whispered in my ear
warning me
of what happens
to those whose focus
is stuck in the past,
while an architect of Bavel
reminded me
to have reasonable goals
when building
for the future
which Yochanan ben Zakai
cautioned
must adapt
to unforeseen changes.

Just Ask

If you need help,
just ask.
Take the scary step
beyond the threshold
and let your voice
rise up from the depths.
Recognize
when you are on the outside
of yourself
and let others
toss you the lifesaver
you think you don't need
to bring you
not just a slice of bread
but a chance
to once again
eat at the king's table.

 Suzanne Brody

Becoming Myself

Graduate Footsteps

In my central isolation
peering around the blankets
and getting tangled
in demons
forgetting
others are out there
ready to hold me
and lift me up.
Slowly
shedding layers
under the sun
realizing
I am not alone
on the beach.

Organic Continuity

We weave together
long lasting threads of the past
now a new blanket.

Spiritually Dehydrated

The soul slowly awakes
finding itself
gently nourished
in an oasis
of understanding
by those who recognized
all that was needed
was spiritual water.

 Suzanne Brody

Ideal Transition

An ideal transition
pulls me out of the muck
lets me shine again
like the diamond I want to be
spreading sprays of rainbows
sharing my gifts
touching hearts
and watering souls.

Professional Development

I
reclaim
Me,
a majestic miracle.
I
reject
jailers,
create
a castle
I
merit.

          Suzanne Brody

Legal Identity

Who you are
in your heart and mind
doesn't have to match
the boxes on legal forms
and I respect and love
all
of who you are
even in those moments
when I ask
that together
we respect the box.

Natural Balm

I want to capture
the warm wind
wrapping me
in a breezy shawl
and the sounds of the kisses
as water meets shore,
medicine that with time
smooths away
the jagged edges of pain.

 Suzanne Brody

Story of a Name

I'm glad
I wasn't born a boy
to share a name
with a fictional mouse
chosen by a student
I'd never meet
but instead
am linked
to previous generations,
my mother's father
loved so much
his name lives on
in my cousins, too.

Learners Teach

You are teaching me
who you are
and how your brain grows
with every response
to a picture in a book,
question asked
or unexpected answer.
Each interaction
revealing
one more piece
of the puzzle
that is you.

 Suzanne Brody

Legal Mirror

We see you
in all your glory
and long to embrace
the way you entered the world
with all your parents
doctors and scientists.
We want
to call you by name
whatever it might be,
honor the titles
passed down from your ancestors
and pepper our conversations
with your proper pronouns
even in a gendered language.

Assignment

My soul teacher once asked
for a list
impossibly long
of seven to eleven
gifts
given like manna
but squirreled away
among my insecurities.
She coaxed me
to bring them forth
to the light of day
and asked
what I needed
from the world
to share them.
One by one
they danced
across the page,
played peek-a-boo
and hide-and-seek
elusive
even now.

          Suzanne Brody

Foremothers

In heels and hiking boots
they saw a path
where none had been
and wore it smooth,
stepping through holes
turned into doorways,
becoming pathfinders
so all I had to do
was knock
to find a way.

Modern Challenge

The sparks are not there
to be gathered,
they are there
to be nurtured
and hurled out
into the world
to ignite more souls.

 Suzanne Brody

Access Ramps

Create access ramps,
multiple paths
for everyone
to find a way
according to temperament
or passion.
Create some ramps
curvy
lined with flowers,
some steep and straight,
others running parallel
for miles,
or wrapping over and under
before joining
the flow of traffic
that eddies and swirls
pulsing
with life
and meaning.

Torah Spa

Suffuse your life
with Torah,
luxuriate in it
like a bubble bath
with ideas
frothing like steam,
wrap yourself in it
like the fluffy comfort
of a warm towel,
let its scents
settle in every crevice
like the mist of perfume
spritzed in the air,
around you
everywhere you go.

 Suzanne Brody

Rebbe

She is a window
into a world
where we all
walk hand-in-hand with God
and our actions are propelled
by ancient words
whispering in our ears
with messages
that match the unique
patterns of our souls.
She is a window
that opens
our own possibilities within
and gives us wings
made of her own
gossamer memories.
She is the window
to which I return
over and over.

Royal Blue Thread

We set out
in search
of the color of the sky
a way
to hold on
to the infinite,
clasp
a security blanket
reminding us
of love and safety.
Instead we found
ourselves lost
in the depths of the sea
trailing
flashes of blue
between our fingertips.

　　　　　　Suzanne Brody

Autumn Race

We are running
a marathon
across calendar pages
through the peaks
of regret and repentance
hope and promises
erecting shelters of joy
as we blow out
one more candle
surrounded
by the surprise
of family
and today
I pause
hands on knees
breathing in bursts
of preparation
for climbing a mountain
to dance with a gift
we slowly unfold
all year long.

The Narrative Before

Before everything began
was the word,
the story
that breathed life
into us
and bound us
Together.
The narrative
pulses in our veins,
winds its way
across synapses
and fills
the spaces between us.

 Suzanne Brody

Meeting Anatoly Kaplan

A brain externalized
in layers of images
folded into meanings,
coded messages,
a dialogue
between past and present
turning
private into public
when particular
becomes universal.

Transition

The pieces in the kaleidoscope
have been jostled
and suddenly
my tears are mixed with Moses'
and the colors of our hearts
are bathed
in a blue sense of loss
mixed with red hot anger
and clear glimpses
of deep purple pain
at the precipice
separated
from the people we've cared for.

                    Suzanne Brody

Acknowledgements

A special thank you to my students, colleagues and teachers. My gratitude to JEA, MTEI, CJLS, and Pardes SELFies for providing inspiration. I hope when you read these poems, it will spark memories of us working and learning together.

Most importantly, thank you to my family for believing in me, cheering me on, and lifting me up.

About the Author

Rabbi Suzanne Brody is the author of five books of poetry and one novella: Dancing in the White Spaces (2007), Etz Chayim She: Modern Poems Grown from Ancient Texts (2015), Mermaid Tears (2020), Lunch with Rav Dimi (2021), Unearthed (2022), and Serah's Secrets (2022). Her poetry has also featured in newsletters, prayer books, and conference summaries. A graduate of Wellesley College, Suzanne also has a PhD in neuroscience, and received rabbinic ordination from the Ziegler School of Rabbinic Studies in Los Angeles, CA. Her writing is infused with her passion for her family, education, and Judaism. In addition to writing, Suzanne has worked in both formal and informal educational settings, designed and taught numerous courses, participates in the Rabbinical Assembly's Committee on Jewish Laws and Standards, and serves as a JEA (Jewish Educator's Assembly) Board Member.

The Jewish Poetry Project

jpoetry.us

Ben Yehuda Press

From the Coffee House of Jewish Dreamers: Poems of Wonder and Wandering and the Weekly Torah Portion by Isidore Century

"Isidore Century is a wonderful poet. His poems are funny, deeply observed, without pretension." —*The Jewish Week*

The House at the Center of the World: Poetic Midrash on Sacred Space by Abe Mezrich

"Direct and accessible, Mezrich's midrashic poems often tease profound meaning out of his chosen Torah texts. These poems remind us that our Creator is forgiving, that the spiritual and physical can inform one another, and that the supernatural can be carried into the everyday."
—Yehoshua November, author of *God's Optimism*

we who desire: Poems and Torah riffs by Sue Swartz

"Sue Swartz does magnificent acrobatics with the Torah. She takes the English that's become staid and boring, and adds something that's new and strange and exciting. These are poems that leave a taste in your mouth, and you walk away from them thinking, what did I just read? Oh, yeah. It's the Bible."
—Matthue Roth, author, *Yom Kippur A Go-Go*

Open My Lips: Prayers and Poems
by Rachel Barenblat

"Barenblat's God is a personal God—one who lets her cry on His shoulder, and who rocks her like a colicky baby. These poems bridge the gap between the ineffable and the human. This collection will bring comfort to those with a religion of their own, as well as those seeking a relationship with some kind of higher power."
—Satya Robyn, author, *The Most Beautiful Thing*

Words for Blessing the World: Poems in Hebrew and English by Herbert J. Levine

"These writings express a profoundly earth-based theology in a language that is clear and comprehensible. These are works to study and learn from."
—Rodger Kamenetz, author, *The Jew in the Lotus*

Shiva Moon: Poems by Maxine Silverman

"The poems, deeply felt, are spare, spoken in a quiet but compelling voice, as if we were listening in to her inner life. This book is a precious record of the transformation saying Kaddish can bring."
—Howard Schwartz, author, *The Library of Dreams*

is: heretical Jewish blessings and poems by Yaakov Moshe (Jay Michaelson)

"Finally, Torah that speaks to and through the lives we are actually living: expanding the tent of holiness to embrace what has been cast out, elevating what has been kept down, advancing what has been held back, reveling in questions, revealing contradictions."
—Eden Pearlstein, aka eprhyme

Texts to the Holy: Poems
by Rachel Barenblat

"These poems are remarkable, radiating a love of God that is full bodied, innocent, raw, pulsating, hot, drunk. I can hardly fathom their faith but am grateful for the vistas they open. I will sit with them, and invite you to do the same."
—Merle Feld, author of *A Spiritual Life*

The Sabbath Bee: Love Songs to Shabbat
by Wilhelmina Gottschalk

"Torah, say our sages, has seventy faces. As these prose poems reveal, so too does Shabbat. Here we meet Shabbat as familiar housemate, as the child whose presence transforms a family, as a spreading tree, as an annoying friend who insists on being celebrated, as a woman, as a man, as a bee, as the ocean."
—Rachel Barenblat, author, *The Velveteen Rabbi's Haggadah*

All the Holes Line Up: Poems and
Translations by Zackary Sholem Berger

"Spare and precise, Berger's poems gaze unflinchingly at—but also celebrate—human imperfection in its many forms. And what a delight that Berger also includes in this collection a handful of his resonant translations of some of the great Yiddish poets." —Yehoshua November, author of *God's Optimism* and *Two World Exist*

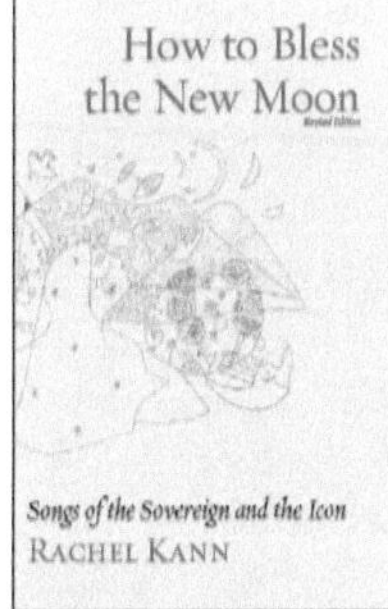

How to Bless the New Moon:
Songs of the Sovereign and the Icon
by Rachel Kann

"Rachel Kann is a master wordsmith. Her poems are rich in content, packed with life's wisdom and imbued with soul. May this collection of her work enable more of the world to enjoy her offerings."
—Sarah Yehudit Schneider, author of *You Are What You Hate*

Into My Garden
by David Caplan

"The beauty of Caplan's book is that it is not polemical. It does not set out to win an argument or ask you whether you've put your tefillin on today. These gentle poems invite the reader into one person's profound, ambiguous religious experience."
—*The Jewish Review of Books*

Between the Mountain and the Land is the Lesson: Poetic Midrash on Sacred Community by Abe Mezrich

"Abe Mezrich cuts straight back to the roots of the Midrashic tradition, sermonizing as a poet, rather than idealogue. Best of all, Abe knows how to ask questions and avoid the obvious answers."
—Jake Marmer, author, *Jazz Talmud*

NOKADDISH: Poems in the Void
by Hanoch Guy Kaner

"A subversive, midrashic play with meanings—specifically Jewish meanings, and then the reversal and negation of these meanings."
—Robert G. Margolis

An Added Soul: Poems for a New Old Religion
by Herbert J. Levine

"Herbert J. Levine's lovely poems swing wide the double doors of English and Hebrew and open on the awe of being. Clear and direct, at ease in both tongues, these lyrics embrace a holiness unyoked from myth and theistic searching."
—Lynn Levin, author, *The Minor Virtues*

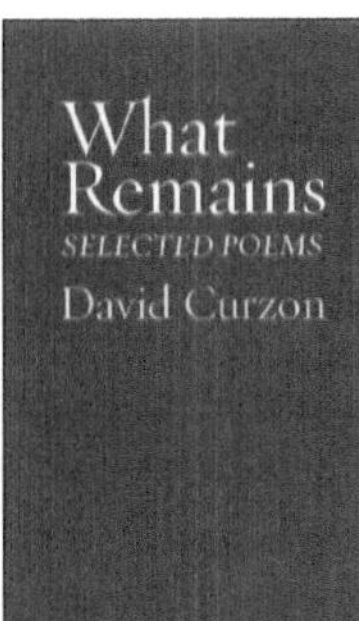

What Remains
by David Curzon

"Aphoristic, ekphrastic, and precise revelations animate WHAT REMAINS. In his stunning rewriting of Psalm 1 and other biblical passages, Curzon shows himself to be a fabricator, a collector, and an heir to the literature, arts, and wisdom traditions of the planet."
—Alicia Ostriker, author of *The Volcano and After*

The Shortest Skirt in Shul
by Sass Oron

"These poems exuberantly explore gender, Torah, the masks we wear, and the way our bodies (and the ways we wear them) at once threaten stable narratives, and offer the kind of liberation that saves our lives."
—Alicia Jo Rabins, author of *Divinity School*, composer of *Girls In Trouble*

Walking Triptychs
by Ilya Gutner

These are poems from when I walked about Shanghai and thought about the meaning of the Holocaust.

Book of Failed Salvation
by Julia Knobloch

"These beautiful poems express a tender longing for spiritual, physical, and emotional connection. They detail a life in movement—across distances, faith, love, and doubt."
—David Caplan, author, *Into My Garden*

Daily Blessings:
Poems on Tractate Berakhot
by Hillel Broder

"Hillel Broder does not just write poetry about the Talmud; he also draws out the Talmud's poetry, finding lyricism amidst legality and re-setting the Talmud's rich images like precious gems in end-stopped lines of verse."
—Ilana Kurshan, author of *If All the Seas Were Ink*

The Missing Jew: Poems 1976-2022
by Rodger Kamenetz

"How does Rodger Kamenetz manage to have so singular a voice and at the same time precisely encapsulate the world view of an entire generation (also mine) of text-hungry American Jews born in the middle of the twentieth century?"
—Jacqueline Osherow, author, *Ultimatum from Paradise* and *My Lookalike at the Krishna Temple: Poems*

The Red Door: A dark fairy tale told in poems
by Shawn Harris

"THE RED DOOR, like its poet author Shawn C. Harris, transcends genres and identities. It is an exploration in crossing worlds. It brings together poetry and story telling, imagery and life events, spirit and body, the real and the fantastic, Jewish past and Jewish present, to spin one tale."
—Einat Wilf, author, *The War of Return*

The Matter of Families
by Robert Deluty

"Robert Deluty's career-spanning collection of New and Selected poems captures the essence of his work: the power of love, joy, and connection, all tied together with the poet's glorious sense of humor. This book is Deluty's masterpiece."
—Richard M. Berlin, M.D., author of *Freud on My Couch*

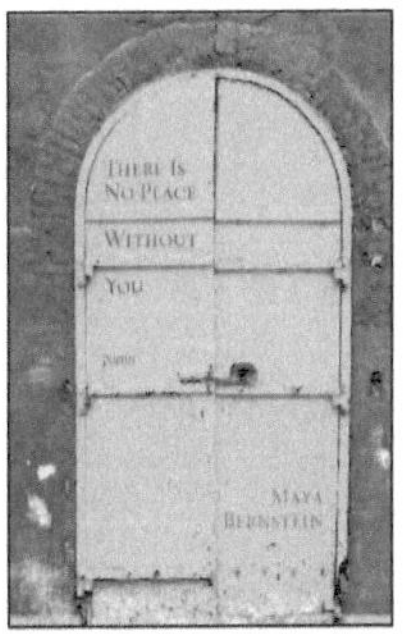

There Is No Place Without You
by Maya Bernstein

"Bernstein's poems brim with energy and sound, moving the reader around a world mapped by motherhood, contemplation, religion, and the effects of illness on the body and spirit. Her language is lyrical, delicate, and poised; her lens is lucid and original."
—Anthony Anaxagorou, author of *After the Formalities*

Torah Limericks
by Rhonda Rosenheck

"Rhonda Rosenheck knows the Hebrew Bible, and she knows that it can stand up to the sometimes silly, sometimes snarky, but always insightful scholarship packed into each one of these interpretive jewels."
—Rabbi Hillel Norry

Words for a Dazzling Firmament
by Abe Mezrich

"Mezrich is a cultivated craftsman: interpretively astute, sonically deliberate, and spiritually cunning."

—Zohar Atkins, author of *Nineveh*

Everything Thaws
by R. B. Lemberg

"Full of glacier-sharp truths, and moments revealed between words like bodies beneath melting permafrost. As it becomes increasingly plain how deeply our world is shaped by war and climate change and grief and anger, articulating that shape feels urgent and necessary."
—Ruthanna Emrys, author of *A Half-Built Garden*

Bits and Pieces
by Edward Pomerantz

"A stunning tapestry of family life in the 40s and 50s. Like all great poetry, Pomerantz's work expands after reading. Each poem is exquisitely structured, often with a stunning ending, into a masterful whole."
—Alan Ziegler, editor of *SHORT: An International Anthology*

Old Shul
by Pinny Bulman

"Nostalgia gives way to a tender theology, a softly chuckling illumination from within the heart of/as a beautiful, broken sanctuary, somehow both gritty and fragile, grimy and iridescent – not unlike faith itself."
—Jake Marmer, author of *Cosmic Diaspora*

Poems for a Cartoon Mouse
by Andrew Burt

"Andrew Burt's poetry magnifies the vanishingly small line between danger and safety. This collection asks whether order is an illusion that veils chaos, or vice-versa, juxtaposing images from the Bible with animated films."
—Ari Shapiro, host of NPR's *All Things Considered*

Feet In L.A., But My Womb Lives In Jerusalem, My Breath In Vermont
by Lori Levy

"Reading through Lori Levy's new book of poems takes my breath away. With no pretense whatsoever, they leap, alive, from the page until this reader felt as if she were living Levy's life. How does the author do it?"
—Mary Jo Balistreri, author of *Still*

Ode to the Dove: *An illustrated, bilingual edition of a Yiddish poem by Abraham Sutzkever*
Zackary Sholem Berger, translator
Liora Ostroff, Illustrator

"An elegant volume for lovers of poetry."
—Justin Cammy, translator of *Sutzkever, From the Vilna Ghetto to Nuremberg: Memoir and Testimony*

poem hashavua: A Personal Engagement with the Weekly Torah Portion in Poems and Pictures
by Lexie Botzum et al.

"Giving voice to unarticulated interpretations and stories, weaving yourself into the text, is a way of claiming ownership."
—from the author's Introduction

Duets on Psalms:
Drawing New Meaning From Ancient Words
by Jack Riemer & Elie Spitz
"Two remarkable rabbis breathe new life into the ancient words of The Book of Psalms. A literary journey filled with faith, wisdom, hope, healing, meaning and inspiration."
—Rabbi Naomi Levy, author of *Einstein and the Rabbi and To Begin Again*

Chrysalis Summer: Poems of Transformation
by Suzanne Brody
"Each page offers a unique surprise. Each poem, with its own unique flavor, elicits a distinct feeling ranging from sweet, amused wonderings to spicy cries of frustration, pain, and longing, to simply savory, enjoyable nuggets. The thoughts and emotions of one woman who plays many roles—teacher, mother, rabbi, and artist."
—Dori Weinstein, author of the YaYa & YoYo series"

So Many Warm Words
Selections from the Poetry of Rosa Nevadovska

A bilingual edition of Yiddish poems
translated by Merle L. Bachman